Rana's Collection

UI LUKKO NÜÑ-2

Folk Tales of Apatani of Ziro Valley, Arunachal Pradesh

GYATI RANA

BlueRose ONE.com
Stories Matter
NewDelhi • London

BLUEROSE PUBLISHERS
India | U.K.

BlueRose ONE.com
Stories Matter
NewDelhi • London

For permissions requests or inquiries regarding this publication,
please contact:

BLUEROSE PUBLISHERS
www.BlueRoseONE.com
info@bluerosepublishers.com
+91 8882 898 898
+4407342408967

ISBN: 978-93-7018-545-6

Cover design: Yash Singhal
Typesetting: Namrata Saini
Illustrators: Artist Bamin Tangu and Artist Kago Laliyang

First Edition: March 2025

Dedication

I dedicate this book to all Indigenous peoples practising their ancient culture and traditions with love and dedication.

Acknowledgement

The tales presented in this book are compiled from the Apatani oral tradition called Miji-Miguñ.

Miji-miguñ, the oral tradition of Apatani refers to a body of knowledge that is vast like the universe itself, wherein metaphysics and cosmology like the creation of the universe, celestial bodies, elements, spirits, living beings, vegetation and the human struggle for survival, its relationship with spirits, elements, vegetation etc. and the world view of Apatani is enshrined.

This book has a rich history and stems from my extensive consultations and interactions with esteemed knowledgeable elders, skilled folklorists, Nyibus (Shamans), and numerous other friends over my two decades of cultural activism. My deepest gratitude goes out to all those individuals, whether named or unnamed, who have played a vital role, both directly and indirectly, in the creation of this book.

I offer my sincere thanks, filled with reverence, to my revered elders – Sri Gyati Tajo, Sri Gyati Taming, Sri Hage Halyang, Sri Mudang Pai, Sri Talyang Halley, and Hage Apa, all of whom are repository of oral tradition miji-migun and esteemed Shamans (Nyibu) and folklorists within the Apatani community, which serves as my primary source of our rich oral literature. Their generous contributions of narratives on folklore and oral traditions have been invaluable to the development of this book.

Furthermore, I extend my heartfelt appreciation to the Artist of Bamin Art Studio, Shri Bamin Tangu and Shri Kago

Laliyang who graciously volunteered their time and talents to illustrate this book, enhancing its appeal and providing readers with a captivating visual experience.

Author

Introduction

Ui lukko niiñ-2 is my second book of folktales compiled from Miji-Miguñ, the oral tradition of Apatani. It continues to explore the rich cultural tapestry of the Apatani community in Ziro Valley, delving into the tales from Miji-Miguñ, the oral tradition of Apatani are folk tales and lores known in Apatani language as, "Ui Lukkò niiñ or Miguñ. The stories I have compiled in this book encompass myths, folklore, and mythology, enshrined as Miji-Migun. It is passed down through generations and offers a deeper understanding of the community's traditions culture, values ethos, heritage and world views.

Despite variances in narratives among different villages and clans, the core themes and objectives of the tales remain consistent. As this compilation of narrations from various sources, like Nyibu, and Popi Sarmin of different villages is acquainted to me, it may not align with every individual's perspective. But it would encourage readers to appreciate the diversity inherent in our oral tradition; miji-migun and oral literary culture.

While some stories may not fit the conventional definition of folk tales, they carry cultural significance and have been widely embraced by the Apatani community as part of their folk tale heritage.

This collection of tales invites readers to immerse themselves in the timeless wisdom and traditions of the Apatani people.

Author

Preface

This book "Ui Lukko Niiñ-2" is the continuation of my compilation of lore and folk tales of Apatani of my previous folktale compiled in "Ui Lukko Niin-1. Like the earlier one, this book also has a collection of twelve stories that delve into the lore and tales of the Apatani people. These stories have been gathered from Nyibu, Shaman, and Popi Sarmin, scholars of the oral traditions of the Apatani community.

The first chapter, "Hulu," deals in depth with the philosophical subject of the origin of knowledge and wisdom called miji-miguñ. The narration begins with the birth of Charun, the God of wisdom and divine knowledge Miji-migun. It explores how Charun, initially unaware of his divinity, evolved into a deity revered for his wisdom and knowledge. How and to whom he imparted his wisdom and divine knowledge; the art of living and expression to different living beings and elements.

The tale of Shu-Myoro, a Terrestrial God in the Apatani belief system, sheds light on the origins of this deity and its relationship with Abotani and his descendants. It digs into how they sustain us while protecting the environment, vegetation, humans, and animals.

The story in Miching Milying Lemba touches upon Abotani's journey into a surreal realm and a mysterious village inhabited by spirits and cannibals.

The Third Eye of Abotani delves into his struggle for survival among adversary spirits who were conspiring against him and the evolution of the festival of reconciliation known as Myoko, the main festival of Apatani.

Other stories in the book include the saga of Aro Donii and Yama Donii, the first agriculturists among the Apatani people, the legend of the solar eclipse, and the transformation of Karin Dacha from a poor man to a wealthy and respected individual through sheer dedication and faith to the Yulo deity. The story of Ayo Yamyang tells us why we should respect and practice our traditional customs.

The stories of Pagañ-Lalyañ, Pali-lango, and Ziro Miyu highlight the ancestral ties of the Apatani people to their land and the measures taken to protect it from envious neighbouring tribes. Additionally, the book explores the origins and evolution of Ovomancy and haruspicy traditions within Apatani society.

I strongly emphasise the importance of preserving native languages as they hold the true cultural essence of a community. While the stories in the book have been translated into English to reach a wider audience, I acknowledge the linguistic and cultural differences between Apatani and English, which may have affected the true essence of the tales from Miji-Miguñ and folk tales. Nevertheless, I hope that the translated stories will provide insight into the Indigenous faith, culture, and traditions of the Apatani people for both young readers and outsiders

Gyati Rana

Contents

CHAPTER-1

Hulu
Permeation of Divine Art and Knowledge

The concept of Hulu in the Apatani language signifies the permeation of divine art and knowledge known as Miji-Miguñ, which plays a crucial role in the beliefs and practices of the Indigenous Apatani ethnic group of Ziro Valley.

The Apatani oral tradition talks about the creation of the Universe by the greater Spirit Ui, and the birth of vegetation, animals, and humans by Nguntü Anii, the mother of Creation. However, these beings were in a "Lyima pücha, Goma Püya", a state without any divine art and knowledge traits. So, they needed to be imbued with sacred knowledge and art known as Miji-Miguñ through a process called "Hulu,".

To permeate the divine art and knowledge within these beings, the Almighty initiated a transformative creation process called "Tapyu Lusi Lusi Anü tiirañ," which resulted in the birth of Aato Charuñ as the infuser and custodian God of Knowledge and wisdom.

But initially, Aato Charuñ too was unaware of his true potential. So, to awaken and activate his latent potential Aato Charuñ. He was gradually pervaded by the divine consciousness known as Aha Büri Kai and Büra Kanya, through a series of divine entities like Aha Jisu and Aha

Gonsu, Aha Jima and Aha Goma, Aha Jidu and Gondu, and Aha Chochañ and Lyolyañ influencing and instilling knowledge within one another permeated it to Aato Charuñ who underwent a profound transformation. From being an unassuming and unknowing entity, he emerged as a vocal, prudent, and wise Custodian God capable of imparting divine knowledge and wisdom to all living beings.

Under the guidance and watchful eyes of Aha Büri Kai and Büra Kanya, Aato Charuñ began to permeate various forms of divine knowledge and arts to the vegetation, animals, and humans inhabiting his domain known as Charuñ be'pü. The first lucky recipients of Charuñ's teachings were Bordi, the Cobra, Dorlañ, the earthworm, and Tü'do, the frog. These beings were bestowed with Chochañ and Lyolyañ, the vocal arts of melody filling their surroundings with enchanting voices.

As Charuñ continued to bestow his wisdom upon various beings in various domains, including insects, animals, and birds, a complex web of knowledge and artistry began to be intertwined with the fabric of life in all living beings.

Alyo Koñso, the Mentis, in the domain called Chaha and, in the realm, called Doha, Doha gulyo, Arki Rünü, Lililiañ, the Cicada and Barbe Yaya Charuñ permeated divine art in their armpit. In the domains of Asañ-Aha; the Süto Nyibu, and Perē Nyibu, the Shamans' divine knowledge was intricately woven into their essence of existence.

At the domain called Lalyi-Yorgo, Takhu, the jungle fowl and in the realm of Lümiñ-Lüpēr, Charuñ infused the vocal art to Kampu and Kanda, the Cranes and Storks respectively to sing around.

Chantuñ, Mother Earth was permeated with Nguru by Charuñ to evolve and maintain the geographical features, seasons and climates to sustain and support living beings. At Dimiñ-pulyañ and Süra-Yorlo, the vegetative area of the Earth, Khonkhuñ, the Eagle was imbued with Pyuli (voice) and Paatü, the Tiger was imbued with Gunga (roar). Among the Tachañ, the worms, Yassañ Tiyo, the woodworms were permeated with divine art and knowledge.

At Dimiñ- pulyañ and Süra-Yorlo, the vegetative area of the Earth, Khonkhuñ, the Eagle was imbued with Pyuli (voice) and Paatu, the Tiger was imbued with Gunga(roar) Among the Tachan, the worms, Yssañ Tiyo, the woodworms were permeated with divine art and knowledge.

In the Domain of Humans, Aato Charuñ's divine knowledge and hymns were intricately woven into Chanjañ and Dotu, the shamans. And amongst the Ui, the Spirits, Charuñ permeated divine knowledge to Ui Lonü, Lyarü Tabyü and Lyantü Potü, the Shamans of spiritual realms. In realm of Nitiñ-Hormiñ, Charun infused Proverbs and Aphorisms to Tabyü-Jirü and Tarsi-Berü. In the realm of

Pümü, the meditation, Charuñ imparted divine art and knowledge to Ashañ Dotu and Aha Penji, the shamans of northern and southern land.

The divine knowledge of affluence was given to Dulu Karngu and Düla Karge; health and Physical strength to Achi Kharü, Anya Khatü, Palo Radhe and Malo Radhe. Expertise in hunting was taught to Miguñ Chatuñ and Mirè Chada. Thus, Aato Charuñ taught and imbued the divine knowledge and Arts to various living beings on this earth under the watchful eyes of Büri Kai and Büra Kanya, who reside in his mind as conscience and morality.

However, not all beings were fortunate enough to receive the divine knowledge and arts from Aato Charuñ. Some, like Sütiñ-Küyi, the Bear, Siiré Pamér, the wild boars, and certain birds and fowls like, Akho Tawu and Ralo-Pagyu, Pügya-Goma and Püwo-Goma, were left behind without any traits from Charuñ. Humans those who were created in the spiritual realm called Adu and Akhu remained unskilled in communications in matters of divine knowledge miji-miguñ.

In the domains of vegetation, among the trees; Dürañ Sañkhañ, Takhé and Sangkiñ Büliñ were not blessed with any traits. Among grasses, the Tami-Kümér and Nüji-Kümér were not imbued with any qualities by Charuñ.

Santu Chopo, the bird, was bestowed with divine knowledge (miji-miguñ) and a melody trait (Chochañ) by Aato Charun. He was revered in the avian realm for his wisdom and beautiful song. However, he became arrogant and proclaimed himself superior to Aato Charun. Upon learning this, Aato Charun revoked all the knowledge and traits he had granted to Santu Chopo. From then on, Santu Chopo, who once sang so beautifully, could only mumble "Popo-Popo".

The tale involving proud Santu Chopo is a cautionary tale that highlights the importance of humility and respect towards those who impart knowledge and wisdom. The story serves as a reminder of the consequences of pride and arrogance, urging beings to approach divine knowledge with reverence and gratitude.

The teachings of Aato Charuñ and the permeation of divine art and knowledge play one of the main roles in shaping the beliefs, practices, and understanding of the Apatani belief system. The intricate web of knowledge and artistry intertwines every aspect of life, guiding beings towards a deeper awareness of their purpose and interconnectedness within the Universe.

CHAPTER-2

Aba Shu-Myoro, The Terrestrial Gods

Within the realm of Apatani lore, the divine entity Ui is said to have manifested as Aba Shu and Aba Myoro, two terrestrial deities tasked with overseeing the flourishing of the environment, vegetation, and living beings. Their creation through the transformative process known as "Cha Kanku Anü Türang" underscores their pivotal role in the spiritual fabric of Apatani belief leading a cadre of subordinate deities called "Shu Dolo," such as *Pahü Nyimuñ, Pa Miha, Dibü Chirrü, Rungo Choro, Tatiñ Kibo, Tayo Ro'po, Jilyu Tuki, Yange Mija, Shu Lyatu, Myoro lyago, Popér Nyimuñ, Raja Miha, Rubo Takhü, Ruttér Yapér* and *dolo haley.* Aba Shu and Aba Myoro exercise authority in supervising the surrounding environs, ensuring the vitality of the organic world and the welfare of the inhabitants dwelling therein.

Within the realm of Apatani lore, the divine entity Ui is said to have manifested as Aba shu and Aba Myoro, two terrestrial deities tasked with overseeing the flourishing of the environment, vegetation and living being.

When Abotani, the legendary ancestor of the Apatani people, planned to migrate from the sacred place of Müdo Pyagañ Poro, the Aba Shu and Aba Myoro expressed their heartfelt desire to accompany him. Initially, Abotani declined but when Aato Shu and Aba Myoro told him they were assigned to oversee the environment, vegetation, animals and living beings and would protect, sustain and bless them with many offspring. Later, Abo Tani agreed to migrate with him under the condition that they would dwell on the outskirts of the village and refrain from causing any harm to the people.

Aba Shu, mindful of his duty to protect the land, warned Abotani that if anyone trespasses into his domain and causes harm while working in the gardens or constructing their houses, he would retaliate. Abotani thought that accidental trespassing may occur due to ignorance of his descendants and they could not harbour enmity for eternity. So, he asked "We cannot culture grudges against each other for eternity. How shall we reconcile? Aba Shu and Aba Myoro proposed a rite involving offerings of eggs and fowls, similar to the one that had reconciled the deities like Aato Ganchi-Galañ and Amiñ-Ganko in the past.

From that moment onwards, Shu-Myoro migrated alongside the descendants of Abotani, resided on the outskirts of settlements, under the shade of big trees, and in other significant places. They diligently oversaw the habitat and environment, blessed the people with children and domestic animals, and safeguarded them from epidemics, calamities, and premature deaths, ensuring their continuous growth and prosperity for generations.

Therefore, the Apatani people, knowing the vital role played by Aba Shu and Aba Myoro in their lives, propitiate them compulsively during festivals and ceremonies. Additionally, if a family member ever falls ill, they seek guidance from an oracle using eggs or chicken liver and perform rituals to appease the deities. Each village in the Ziro Valley has a designated place for worshipping Shu-Myoro, indicating their deep reverence and gratitude for the Gods who watched over them and ensured their well-being and prosperity.

An excerpt from the hymns of the Shu-Myoro ritual with English translation is given below:

Aba shu-Aba Myoro !
Talii chago mi shu ali tuggo bipe,
Neli to'ggo mi myoro ala la'go bipe
Bünü Sunü mi Dimpu Momu
Miló Sunü mi Hikhüñ chinchiñ sugü pe

Assañ dalyi alyi mudu laho tope,
Aha dalyi arro miie lapa tope,
Dachañ müdu Ürrii müdu laho bipe
Kojiñ miidu Pülañ müdu laho bipe

Riichi Taju mi Rulyu dopa suggi pe,
Khemyo tayu mi rulyu dopa sugii pe.
Ro'pò Sunüñ Müğañ sarda sugii pe
Lyipo sunüñ Hipo toto sugii pe

Sübo sunüñ Ri Tara sugii pe
Aba shu dichan alya mi lyantii lyanto pe
Aba Myoro liidi ango mi goro goto pe

Oh, Father Shu and Myoro the divine,
Guard us from death's untimely chime,
Shield us from Neli and Talii's veil,
Guide us to maturity beyond the pale.
Sustain the women till their hair grows grey
Nourish the men till their teeth drops away

Protect us from the North's fierce storms,
And the South's swirling cyclones in alarm,
Preserve us from cold's biting breath,
And the heat's scorching kiss of death.
Watch over us in fire's dangerous dance,

Let our sons and daughters thrive and enhance,
May our Cocks strut with pride and grace,
Our Pigs with teeth like swords in their face.

May our Mithuns grow strong and tall,
With horns that rise like a mighty wall,
Aba Shu, sustain us in eternity's embrace,
Aba Myoro, shield us with your grace.

CHAPTER -3

The Mystic Eye and Spike

The story of Abo Tani and his Third Eye and Spikes delves into the realms of ancient Apatani mythology and folklore, offering insights into the values and beliefs of the indigenous Tani groups.

Abo Tani, the forefather of the Tani people married Hasañ Buluñ Bünyi, the sister of Hasañ Buluñ Mikhü, the god of Strength and Velour. Hasañ Buluñ Mikhün in Mida, the marriage ceremony gifted him an extra eye and spikes as Ma'bo Yalo (Gift to Bride). This tradition of "Mabo Yalo" in Mida, a traditional marriage Ceremony" is still being practised by the Apatani community invariably.

He possessed unique gifts bestowed upon him through his marriage. Koga Mirü, the third eye he adorned at the backside of his head could see into the realms of spirits. This eye granted him knowledge and insight beyond the physical world, enabling him to easily navigate together the realms of the living, Neha and Ui, the spirits. The Lüdu-Pümyi, the powerful spikes in his legs and hands, made him a formidable figure capable of conquering his enemies and adversaries in both realms.

The third eye he adorned at the backside of his head could see into the realms of spirits. This eye granted him knowledge and insight beyond the physical world, enabling him to easily navigate together the realms of the living, Neha and Ui, the spirits.

However, Abo Tani's gifts also triggered his downfall as his ego grew unchecked. He became proud and arrogant, believing himself to be the Lord of both realms. This arrogance ultimately led to a tragic incident where he unintentionally killed Tubo Halye and Lyabo Hakhe, two children of prominent spirits, sparking a vengeful plot against his life by the spirits.

The spirits Tubo, Lyabo and their kins Myotü, Pilya, Dingyañ and Shü sought revenge by luring Abo Tani to a swing on a mythical cliff, intending to eliminate him. When Tani swung up they kept him aloof up in the swing with Bamboo and other spiked poles called *Tabyuñ Tochi* and *Tamo Toko* to let him die. They also dragged his wife *Hassañ Buluñ Bünyi* and pushed her into a well to let her drown in the water. When *Hassañ Buluñ Mikhi,* her brother, came to know this he resurrected her through a ritual called *buluñ hinüñ* and took her back to his abode.

The entire spirits of the realm Ui were against Abotani except for the spirit within, i.e., "Günü Pilya" who was softening the soil below AboTani perchance he might fall and get hurt. Yet, the intervention of the divine entities, namely Almighty Alo and Pontang, the wise elders among the Spirit is a pivotal turning point in the tale.

Divine Alo and Pontang understood that the realm of spirits, Ui and realms of the physical world, Neha, were complimentary to each other like Body and Soul. So, they intervened to prevent Abotani's death. They advocated for compassion and suggested the path of retribution of Abotani's weapons in place of their dead sons. Abo Tani thus undergoes a process of spiritual disarming, surrendering his potent gifts "Koga Mirü, and Lüdu Pümyi" as reconciliation, and atonement.

Such disarmament of his powerful gifts left him frail, ignorant, unaware and vulnerable in the realm of spirits. He often committed mistakes and angered the benevolent spirits of the realm of Ui. Later, he committed mistakes again and due to his ignorance, all the spirits had grudges against Abotani.

Therefore, under the guidance of Popi and the suggestion of his sister, Dolyang Chanjang, Abo Tani evolved Myoko Festival and engaged in rituals and ceremonies to reconcile with the spirits and seek redemption for his mistakes and annoyance caused them.

Hence, the Apatanis celebrate the Myoko Festival every year. They seek forgiveness through offerings in festivals known as Lochi-Hüba and reciprocate their offering of gifts with blessings of the benevolent Spirits, health, wealth and peace and also show the importance of humility, respect, and harmony in relationships with both the physical and spiritual worlds.

In essence, the tale of the Mystic Eye and Spike of Abotani serves as a cautionary reminder of the consequences of unchecked pride and the significance of maintaining balance and reverence in our interactions with the world around us. It highlights the interconnectedness of all beings and the enduring need for humility and respect in navigating the complexities of life and spirituality.

CHAPTER-4

Michiñ Milyiñ Lemba: A Journey to the Enigmatic Village of Spirits and Cannibals

Once Abotani the forefather of Apatani embarked on a hunting expedition like no other. Armed with his snares called "Gürü", placing them where rats tread and birds perch, at his Moore, the hunting track. He constructed "Gümya" a sharp spiked Trap where the Boar, Deer and other big animals' trails to catch them. As he meticulously laid out his traps, little did he know that fate had something extraordinary in store for him.

In the following days, he ventured back to his hunting track to check on his traps. To his astonishment, he found that one of his spiked traps (Gümya) had ensnared a powerful Jungle Boar but it had somehow managed to escape.

He ventured back to his hunting track to check on his traps. To his astonishment, he found that one of his spiked traps (gumya) has ensnared a powerful jungle Boar but it had somehow managed to escape.

He saw blood spots all over the track where the boar moved away. Resolute to track down the injured Beast, he followed the trail of blood that led him deep into a dark and grim cave. Holding a flickering torch, Abotani ventured further into the forbidding dark tunnel, guided only by his unwavering determination. After what seemed like an eternity of navigating through the darkness, he emerged on the other side of the tunnel, only to be greeted by a sight that defied all logic. Before him lay a mystical village, shrouded in mystery and intrigue.

Curious Abotani walked down to the village. When he entered there, he was astonished and intrigued to see his sister on the veranda of a house who had recently died. She also saw Tani curiously walking down the village lane. She came down promptly from the veranda and asked,

"Brother! Why and how have you come to this place?"

"I came here trailing an injured jungle Boar in my trap (Gümya). Tani replied and asked intriguingly. "What are you doing here, you died recently. What and whose village are this?" confused Abotani added.

In a voice filled with echoes of the past, his sister said, "This is the boundary between the living and the dead blurred into a surreal existence where spirits and cannibals roamed freely. After my death, I have been married to a cannibal spirit who can transform into any animal and even a human being."

As Abotani unravelled the mysteries of this otherworldly village, his mind swirled with questions and fears.

"Have you seen any injured boar around here?" Tani asked her sister.

His sister shared chilling tales and told him "I heard one of the residents of this village, Ama Hiruñ was injured by gümya, that boar must be him who got hit by your gümya. Two shamans, Apa Pakhu attired with a necklace of Eggshells, and Apa Miiri attired with a necklace of charcoal are performing a healing ritual at his house." She told him.

Shocked and alarmed Tani halted and listened, he heard, "Tani boka dasañ Kugu, Toro boka ralañ Kaga...." "Ui Barnüñ" hymns emanating from a distant house.

She continued, "Brother, this is the abode of spirits and cannibals, you should return immediately. If they see you, they will eat you up. And if they get your scent, all of them will leave the ritual and come here running to eat you." Frightened sister expressed her apprehension.

Trapped in a web of intrigue and danger, Abotani was on the brink of a precarious situation. With the chilling warnings of his sister ringing in his ears, he did not know how to find a way out of this surreal realm before the spirits and cannibals discovered his presence.

Fearful Tani told his sister, "I am lost and have forgotten the way back,".

His worried sister told him "I will hide you in Aggo Epuñ." She took Tani to the corner of the house, sat him there covered him with a Güda-patta; a big basket and said, "Site here silently whatever situation may be until I think of a way out for you to return to your land."

Tani covered with Güda-Pata sits silently at the corner of the Aggo-Epuñ as told by her sister.

After a while, as expected all the people who were gathered at the ritual performance stopped the performance and came running to that house shouting "Human! Human! Where is the human, the human aroma is coming from my house?" her cannibal husband inquired with salivating mouth.

"Yesterday, I came back from the land of humans, the smell must be coming out from me." She told him casually. They snipped her and went back for the ritual agreeing to her statement.

When people went back for the ritual, her sister told Tani, "Brother if you have forgotten the way back. I have an idea, it is the time for "Lyidü" the spirits of seasonal birds and insects to travel to Neha, your land. You may follow them they will lead you to your land."

As guided by his sister's wisdom, Abotani embarked on a perilous journey to follow the spirits of seasonal birds and insects, the "Lyidü," back to his land of Neha. In the middle of the way, while resting at a "Nyatu" the resting place, the spirits started conversing with each other.

Since they were only in the form of spirits one of them said I would be Lili-lilañ, the Cicada, another said I would be Tüpü-püpü, next said I would be Kakapapo, next said I would be Chipü Yarü, next said I would be Puchuñ-Tachuñ, and next said I would be putér-tatér, next the last one got confused and could not say what he will be. Immediately, they caught him, tore him into pieces, and ate him along with their tiffin.

Having eaten their tiffin, they continued their journey. Again, Tani followed them and reached Neha, his Land and land of living beings. When they reached Neha, he saw that one who claimed to be Lili-lilañ transformed into Cicada and sang lilil lilañ, one who claimed to be Tüpü-püpü transformed into a tüpü-püpü bird and started singing "Tüp pü pü". Kakapapo also transformed into Kakapapo bird and started singing "Kaka Papo". Likewise, all the spirits transformed into different seasonal birds and insects and started singing declaring the arrival of the new season.

Since that day, the Abotani know that Lyidü, the spirits of seasonal birds and insects migrate from the realm of spirits, Neli to Neha. They transform into different seasonal birds and insects and declare the changing seasons guiding their agricultural practices, festivals and traditional ceremonies.

This tale of Michiñ Milyiñ Lemba, the Village of Spirits & Cannibals, continues to be retold by the Apatanis to highlight the importance of respecting and navigating the spiritual world.

CHAPTER-5

Donü, The First Agriculturist

Chantu, the Earth, was formed from celestial dust and water by the Almighty Ui during the early stages of Kolyuñ. It passed through various epochs such as Kolo, Ui, Üpyo Müdo, and Supuñ. When Chantu, the Earth transcended into the Üpyo, Abotani, the first human and our forefather, was born from the womb of Chantu, the Mother Earth. He endured great challenges from the elements and spirits, leading to the growth of his descendants into different tribes and clans. However, these tribes and clans were nomadic, surviving on wild plants, fruits, and edible roots, and hunting for food.

The resource-full and fertile lands were occupied and owned by powerful beings and spirits such as the wild banana Grove, *Kuduñ Byopü,* and *Küpa byolyo* were occupied by the Spirits of Jungle *Doji* and *Lyapuñ.* Lord of Shade and Darkness, Kami-Kamo, owned the Sanchi-pu and Sama-Pu. *Radi-Rahu, Rapa-Raha ganda,* where wild chestnut grows was occupied by *Mingo Donü,* the affluent and powerful among the Donü tribe. The poor Arro-Donü and Yama-Donü had no land to cultivate and only the option to hunt.

One day, while hunting, the Arro-Donü and Yama-Donü observed seeds growing in soils disturbed by wild boars. This inspired them to cultivate by clearing land, hoeing it, and planting seeds to grow more abundant food crops.

They searched for fertile, unoccupied land like -*Müdo Küjiñ byopü, Jilyu madiñ Yoyu mabyañ, Tatü Kokhe, Sopiñ la'pañ,* and *Sübi Kotér.* It was not conducive and cold and saplings could not grow and survive there. Next, they tried the *Tariñ Tanchi* and *Tau Tamér* land and found that it was hubs of various bacteria and viruses. All of them were discarded and finally settled on a fertile land called Dikha atè, Diha abañ, Nyamp tü'kuñ, Pili sekuñ ganda. Though they occupied the land they needed good tools and implements.

So, they embarked upon a trip to distant lands to buy sharp tools and implements. From the land of *Pannü,* they buy the mythical Machete called "Ma'bo Loy'chi". And from the land called *Tugyo,* "Turu Dipe", the mythical hue. While returning home, they sharpen them on the stones at the banks of *Kuru* and *Küme* River.

Again, the erratic climate and weather prevented them from going for cultivation. So, they sought help from *Loma*, the Artisan God. Who taught them how to prepare rain shields and baskets from cane and bamboo. Accordingly, they prepared the Tarpi Yatü, the rain shield and Tassér Barju; the basket. They adorned themselves with Tarpi Yatü to protect themselves from erratic weather. They carried their implements and foods in their Tassér Barju, a basket, and went out for cultivation.

Yet again, the evil spirits of wild vegetation *Pyakuñ Pemo* and *Pyo Tadu* blocked their way with their colossal long hands and legs. So, they went to the mighty warriors *Dulu Talañ* and *Myamya Pükha* and sought their help. On their persuasion, *Dulu Talañ* and *Myamya Pükha* cut off the hands and legs of *Pyakuñ Pemo* and *Pyo Tadu* with their sharp swords, killed them by cutting open their stomach and cleared their way to the cultivation field.

After that, Arro Donü and Yama Donü cut down the wild bushes and trees growing on their selected land and let them dry in the sun. When it became dry, it needed to be burnt down and cleared.

So, they made torches from dry wood and went to the land called Yani-Yana where the jungle fire was burning. They brought the fire from that land, burnt down the dried bushes and trees and prepared the land for jhum cultivation. They had no suitable seed to sow, therefore they searched for the right seeds.

Sources of various Paddy seeds:

When the bone marrow of the Goddess of creation and nourishment; *Hintü Annü* manifested into various paddy. Goddess *Hintü Annü's* elder daughter, *Murtu Yariñ* kept all *Pyapiñ* and *Pyare* variety of Paddy for herself. Her younger daughter, *Hintü La'gér Tachi* took away the Empu and *Elañ* variety of Paddy as a gift in her marriage with *Hirü Tatu* of *Hirü.* There was nothing left for Arro Donü and Yama Donü to sow in their field.

So, *Arro Donü* and Yama Donü went to the land of *Murtu* and persuaded Murtu Yariñ for some seeds but she declined. Then, Arro Donü kidnapped *Murtu Yariñ.* She asked, "We had no issue or dispute, why did you kidnap me?" *Donii* replied, "Yes, we have no dispute, but you declined to give us seeds of *Pyapiñ* and *Pyaré.* You give us the seeds and we will set you free."

Thus, Arro Donü and Yama Donü collected seeds of *Pyapiñ* and *Pyare* Paddy from *Murtu Yariñ*, as ransom for her freedom.

As told earlier, before venturing for cultivation, Arro Donü and Yama Donü were surviving only on wild roots, fruits, leaves, and through hunting. Once, Yama Donü laid snares in his hunting track where rats threaded and caught some rats. He took them to his home while dissecting their stomach to clean them to cook, he found that the stomach of Rat was filled with whitish bolus (ball of half-digested food in the oesophagus and Stomach) indicating that it had eaten Paddy seeds. He was intrigued and thought that he had been surviving on wild leaves and his stomach had a greenish bolus and greenish latrine. How come the Rats have a whitish bolus in their stomach, from where this rat has partaken Paddy seeds?

So, Yama Donü also referred to as *Donü Tani* embarked on an expedition to search and verify the source. He put his pet Dog *Kibo Talo* to pursue the ways where rats had threaded. He followed his Dog who led him to the land of *Hirü.* There he saw a huge Tree called *"Hirü Lyagguñ"*. He also saw rats playing amidst the *Permo* and *Malo* (varieties of Paddy) growing upon the huge branches of that tree covered with algae and Mosses. Yama Donii collected the *Empu* and *Elañ* Paddy seeds from there.

Then, Arro Donü was less inclined towards wet rice cultivation and continued Jhum cultivation with Pyapiñ and Pyaré. Yama Donü being more inquisitive, dedicated himself to trying wet-rice cultivation. He learned the technique of constructing channels, bounds and slashes to harvest water for paddy from Bo'liñ Tatiñ and Süliñ Tamañ, the engineer disciple of Aato Hachañ Pui Hachañ. Subsequently, he prepared nursery beds and sowed *Pyapiñ* and *Pyaré* in one and another bed, Empu and *Elañ.* After some days, it sprouted into the size of a snake's teeth, in the following days it grew into the size of a lizard's tail. After some months it was transplanted into the Paddy field.

When it sprouted into the size of Lizard's tail in the following month it was transplanted into the prepared paddy field.

Then the elements and Spirits started conspiring against them. In an evil creation called "Pungu türañ" the evil Dree and his accomplices; the various pests, termites and harmful microbes were created. The vengeful spirit of *Pyakuñ Pemo* and *Pyo Tadu* who were killed earlier also manifested from their stomach in the form of pests and wild sparrows to take revenge on Arro Donü and Yama Donü.

The evil *Dree* led all these pests, sparrows, microbes and other harmful elements equipped with mythical teeth of "*Pungu Annü*", the evil creator mother to damage whatever Arro Donü and Yama Donü cultivated. So, they were worried about the intent and plan of the evil spirit *Dree* and its accomplices.

So, Arro *Donü* approached *Achi Kharü/Donü Kharü*, the warrior Shaman of the Donü clan and said persuasively, "O, Gallant *Kharü,* the adorner of mythical Spear "dalañ-dambu", mythical bows and arrows *Gelañ-Gembu*", and Mythical shield *Chalañ-Chanko.* Through your gallant expedition, you have earned spoils like mythical Caps "Tai byoduñ" and "Gyara Tagya" from *Dadu Tangu* and *Püo Dara* countries. You have settled and given solutions to various problems of society since eternity. There is no one so gallant and more expert than you who can save us from evil *Dree* and his accomplice. Please help us and save our crops from the evil *Dree* and his accomplices, insects, pests, microbes sparrows, etc., who are conspiring and planning to destroy our crops."

Hearing the urge and prayer of Arro *Donü* and *Yama Donü, Achi Kharü* adorned himself with a cap called *Tassu Byotu,* a sachet called *Tasse Nara* and took his mythical spear, bow and arrow called *Dalañ-Dambu* and *Gelañ Gembu,* respectively, and invoked Metü-Tamu, the warrior God and Medér, the god of purification through a ritual with hymns and offerings. Then, Metü and Tamu killed away the insects and pests and *Medér,* purified the atmosphere and ensured the healthy growth of crops. Thus, the evil *Dree* and his force of pests and microbes were pacified from destroying the crops of *Ane Donü* and *Aba Lübo* in the initial cultivation at the epoch of *Üpyo.*

Since then, Apatani performed "Dree" an agricultural ritual wherein the Warrior God *Metü-Tamu* is invoked and propitiated to pacify evil *Dree* and kill his accomplice, and *Medĕr* to purify the atmosphere to ensure healthy growth of crops and bumper harvests. The performance of this agricultural ritual transcended from iipyo to Miido, from

Miido to Sülo supuñ (Ziro Valley) all along the migration route of Apatani.

The narrative of Donü's agricultural legacy has been ingrained in the cultural fabric of the Apatani tribe. The agriculture practices and rituals established by Donü have transcended time, evolving into a revered pan-Tani agricultural festival in 1967 that celebrates the enduring spirit of agriculture innovation and cooperation. Initially, it was celebrated collectively at Sülañ Ditiñ by the whole Apatani community. But nowadays, it is celebrated in the valley by three groups: at Hija, Sülañ Ditiñ, at Bürü by the whole Hong village alone and Nago Putu by Supuñ, the remaining villages in Ziro Valley.

However, the legend of Donü, the dedicated, innovative and hardworking farmer, continues to be told around the world where Dree Festival is being celebrated through Dree Büsi, Dree Ayu, recalling and explaining the intricate cultivation technique of our forefather Donü and the evolution of agriculture and reminding us of the power of dedication, innovation, determination and teamwork in overcoming challenges in the human life and achieving great things.

CHAPTER-6

Danyi Tatii Arnii Niing; Solar Eclipse

There are varied concepts and beliefs related to the solar eclipse. Every culture and faith have its own explanation. There is mention of various demons and mythical animals who cause the eclipse, e.g., Rahu of Hindus, Dragon of the Chinese, Wolves of Vikings, and so on. The Indigenous Apatani also has its concept and explanation of the solar eclipse. The story goes like this-

Long ago, before the birth of Ayo Danyi, the Sun, this world was under the domain of the Terrestrial God Shu Myoro. When Ayo Danyi, the Sun was born by Goddess Ami Nüdo, the first celestial Woman, Ayo-Danyi, the sun also needed a domain for herself.

So, one day the Terrestrial God, Shu Myoro asked the Sun, *Ayo Danyi*, "Let us work together to sustenance and nourish the lives on this Earth and let us spread our hands and have our domains." *Ayo Danyi* agreed to the proposal and spread her rays all over the Earth, Sky and Universe and terrestrial God, *Shu-Myoro* could spread his hands only at selective places like deep gorges and shaded sides of the hills and mountains.

Therefore, *he* got disappointed and jealous, as he was older than *Üjañ An*ü the Sun, but was left with lesser domains than her. So, he conspired to eliminate her. He allied with *Küe Mutañ Tamu*, the Lord of Strength, Velour and War, and persuaded him to capture and eat up *Danyi* the Sun.

Therefore, in the olden days whenever there happened to be a solar eclipse, while the Nyibu chants Hilan-Hido hymns, the people beat the brass plates and bells to rescue the spirit of the eclipsed sun.

Consequently, *Küei Mutañ Tamu* captured the sun and gulped her into his mouth. Resultantly, darkness and chaos reigned again upon the earth and the sky. The greater spirit, Ui asked *Dolyañ Tachañ*, the celestial Sky Lark, to verify if the sun had died in the captivity of *Tamu.* Accordingly, the sky Lark flayed high up into the sky and met the sun under the captivity of Küei Mutan Tamu. He found that the sun was not yet dead. The sun asked him to rescue her by performing *Hilañ Tuliñ- Hido Pyaliñ,* a ritual to rejuvenate the diminishing spirit and restore physical health.

When it was reported to the Greater Spirit, Ui, the Ui summoned *Üjañ Lyarü-Lyarü Nyibu* to perform the ritual.

Accordingly, *Üjañ Lyarü-Lyarü Nyibu* executed the ritual with water and a bunch of leaves of the chestnut Tree (believed to be Holy and divine) and she was rescued. On her release from the mouth of *Tamu*, the light and orderliness were restored upon the Earth.

Therefore, in the olden days whenever there happened to be a solar eclipse, while the Nyibu chants *Hilañ-Hido* hymns, the people beat the brass plates and bells to rescue the spirit of the eclipsed Sun.

CHAPTER-7

Kariñ Dacha

In the olden days, a poor man lived in a village at Ziro Valley. His name was Kariñ Dacha, he was the poorest among the villagers but was rich in his faith in deities. Whenever there used to be a performance of any ritual or ceremony in his village, he never failed to participate. He was an expert in making Yugyañ (altar) and always gave his helping hand to them. People loved him and always sought him because he was dedicated and used to prepare the Yugyañ beautifully with deep faith and love.

As per the indigenous Apatani belief system, the Goddess Yulo is the Goddess of health, prosperity and affluence. It is held that if someone performs the Yulo ceremony, the Goddess Yulo along with her associate and allied deities shower him with blessings of health and prosperity abundantly. But it is an expensive ritual for the poor and commoners, only affluent people can afford to perform it. However, it is believed that the Yulo Deity has a compassionate and caring heart for the faithful believers, if clan members and villagers participate in the performance of the Yulo ritual with sincerity, dedication and faith they too are blessed equally.

One day, a rich man in the village who was ailing sought an ocular sign of how to get relief from his ailment through ovomancy. After examining the eggs, the wise elders and the Shamans told him to perform the Yulo ceremony to appease the Yulo Deity. Since it was a big event, the decision and the suggestion of wise elders and shamans were made known to every village.

He was an expert in making yugyan (altar) and always gave his helping hand to them. People loved him and always sought him because he was dedicated and used to prepare the yugyan beautifully with deep faith and love.

On the scheduled day of the Yulo ritual, all villagers gathered there to participate in the ceremony. As usual, Kariñ Dacha also came there to help them prepare Yugyañ for the Yulo deity. There were other villagers too who were preparing different parts of Yulo Yugyañ. Kariñ Dacha was asked to prepare the Byoduñ and Chucha (a part of the Yulo Altar shaped like a cap and basket) for the Yulo deity. As usual, Kariñ Dacha happily started preparing the Byoduñ and Chucha with sincerity, dedication, faith and devotion. The ritual ceremony was performed successfully, everyone went back to their home joyously after the final ceremony feast.

Kariñ Dacha also returned to his house happily because such a grand ceremony was rarely performed. He felt as if he had performed the ceremony himself and went to sleep. That night he saw an old lady in his dream who told him, "Dacha, I am happy to receive the Yagü(carrying basket) you prepared for me. It is so beautiful. Surely, I will gift you back appropriately very soon." Kariñ Dacha woke up a bit late and was troubled by his dream. He was thinking who was that unknown Lady in his dream? When did he give her Yagü? What does she want to gift me back?

In our Tradition, the rich man who owns many Mithuns and cows engages other people to look after their Mithun. They were not paid but in the case of female Mithun or cow after every two issues of babies, the third issue goes to the caretaker. Kariñ Dacha and his friend were entrusted to look after on this term to the herds of Mithuns of a rich man.

He got up late that morning and was thinking about his dream, his friend came and asked, "You were always early in searching and caring for the Mithuns, why so late today?"

"I don't know why I am late; I have been dreaming a lot." Kariñ Dacha replied wearily.

"Anyway, I have been in the morning round and saw the Mithun you have been taking care of had given birth to twin baby Mithun." His friend told him and asked. "I think this is the third issue and it will be yours?"

"Yes! This issue is third and would fall in my account" Excited and happy Kariñ Dacha replied.

"Wao! You are lucky, both babies are female." Added his friend.

When this news struck his mind, he realised that the lady he saw in the dream must be Goddess Yulo Anü, he also remembered Byoduñ and the Chucha he prepared at the ceremony and understood that the two Mithun babies were her gift from Yulo goddess. He felt so grateful and thanked the Yulo deity.

Afterwards, Kariñ Dacha also became the owner of two Mithuns. Later when two female Mithuns grew up and gave birth to many more Mithuns Dacha owned a herd of Mithun. He bought many land and other properties in exchange for Mithuns from his herd. And became a rich man in the village with the blessing of the Yulo deity and was respected by all.

Moral: Gods and Goddesses desire true, faith, love and dedication more than any other sacrifice.

CHAPTER-8

Aayo Yamyañ and Benevolent Spirits.

Narrator: Talyang Haley

Traditionally, the Myokó is the main festival of Apatani. The main objectives of the festival are to establish cordial relations with the realm of spirits and to ensure the healthy growth and progression of human beings particularly families, clans and villages by revitalising the relationships in the society and the two realms i.e. Neha, the realms of living beings and Ui, the realms of spirits. It involves the performance of many rituals propitiating the various deities invited from the realms of Spirits followed by observance of certain prescribed taboos.

The celebration of the Myokó festival is hosted every year cyclically by three groups of villages viz Hari-Bula (Hari, Kalung, Reru and Tajang Village), Tünni-Dübo (Hija, Dutta, Mudang Tage and Bamin Michi Village) and Nüchi-Nütü (Hong Village) in Ziro Valley.

Long ago, Aayo Yamyañ an old lady lived alone at the periphery of an Apatani village in Ziro Valley. That year Aayo Yamyañ's village hosted the festival. The festival was celebrated with much pomp and gaiety.

During the festival, the gods and goddesses of the realm of Ui are invited and offered gifts and offerings called Lochi-Hüba. After a month-long celebration at the end of the festival, the deities return to their respective abodes. On that night of "Ui-Alo" a rite is performed wherein Nyibu chants the farewell hymn. As per tradition, the villagers secure their houses with the Takhò (split bamboo) around them to avoid the entry of notorious spirits.

That night, a group of naughty and reluctant spirits benevolent who were late to leave the village after the Myoko festival entered her house, making frightening noises.

Frightened Ayo Yamyan pulled up the blanket and silently listened to their conversations.

Ayo Yamyañ did not care to put Takhò (split bamboo) and secured her house lamenting that she was alone and there was no male member to prepare Takhò for her.

That night, a group of naughty and reluctant spirits benevolent who were late to leave the village after the Myokó festival entered her house, making frightening noises.

Frightened Ayo Yamyañ pulled up the blanket and silently listened to their conversations.

Around the time of the crowing of Cock, a lady spirit gave birth to a child.

An argument started to name the child, some suggested names *Punjirii,* some suggested *Lancha Tara, Yabiñ Tudii, Yalo Tupo* etc. Their argument took too long and before they could agree on a child's name the cock crowed. They knew that dawn was coming so they left the house hurriedly without naming the child.

Aayo Yamyañ was shivering like anything out of fear and couldn't sleep the whole night. This incident shook her deep into the heart. Since then, she never failed to observe the tradition of secluding the house by putting around Takhò at the time of the closing of the Myokó festival.

Moral: Respect and practice the age-old tradition.

CHAPTER-9

How Büsañ Dolyañ, The Most Venomous Snake Lost His Poison.

In the luscious Ziro Valley, home to the Apatani Tribe, the Green Rat Snake, Büsañ Dolyañ, known for his intelligence and agility, coexisted with the sly and mild venomous snake, Büpü-pü'gor.

Initially, Biisañ Dolyañ were the only venomous snake on earth, the deadly poison was obtained from Abañ Chinü, the father of all poisonous beings. Just a portion of a pint of his venom could kill a human instantly. Possessing such potent venom made him haughty and disdainful.

Büsañ Dolyañ often belittled the gentle and non-venomous snakes, Büpü-pü'gor, in-jokes and jests. Fed up with Büsañ Dolyañ's mistreatment, Büpü-pü'gor resolved to teach him a lesson one day.

In the luscious Ziro Valley, home to the Apatani Tribe, the Green Rat Snake, Busan Dolyan, known for his intelligence and agility, coexisted with the sly and mild venomous snake, Bupu- pugor.

One unfortunate day, at a place called Hintü Bugyu, Büsañ Dolyañ, fatally bit a human named Neha Talo, leading to his sudden demise. As Neha Talo's loved ones retrieved his body mourned and performed the final rites, people sang a dirge and bid farewell to the soul of Neha Talo. Biipii-piigor, passing by, overheard the mention of Büsañ Dolyañ's poisonous bite and hatched a plan to humble the venomous snake.

Büpü-Pü'gor approached Büsañ Dolyañ while he was preparing to perform the "Ro'pi" ritual. Büpü-Pü'gor asked innocently,

"Büsang Dolyañ, why this Ro'pi ritual?"

"Today, I fatally bit and killed Neha Talo, hence, I need to subdue his vengeful spirit so that his spirit may not have a chance to take revenge on me." Büsañ Dolyañ replied enthusiastically.

"Ah! It is not necessary! Neha Talo is alive and well, unfazed by your venom. I happened to pass through his house while coming here and I saw him alive. Rather he was performing a Subu ritual as there was a Subu (Mithun) tied at his veranda and even heard his melodious Subu ritual chanting." Büpü-pü'gor lied to him.

"No, it cannot be! My potent venom never fails. Are you joking Büpü-pü'gor?" asked Büsañ Dolyañ warily.

"Yes, Büsañ Dolyañ, you know I never lie, you may go for yourself and verify it," Büpü-pü'gor replied seriously.

Shocked and disbelieved, Büsañ Dolyañ rushed to Neha Talo's residence but dared not approach too closely so that Talo's relative may not avenge him. From a distance, he witnessed the scene described by Büpü-pü'gor – a Mithun tied outside and he could hear the Dirge song but could not understand it from such distance and assume it for the melodic Subu ritual chant. All the ambience he observed from a distance misled him into believing that Neha Talo had survived his deadly attack.

Mortified and alarmed by the uselessness of his venom, Büsañ Dolyañ, convinced of his venom's ineffectiveness, emptied his poison into a gorge. Since then, he has become a vehement yet harmless snake. The remnants of his vomited venoms were eaten by the other snakes and were transformed into venomous snakes.

Legend has it that Pükho, an eagle with fierce features, a descendant of Neha Talo, now hunts snakes as vengeance, a reminder of the consequences of Büsañ Dolyañ's misplaced arrogance.

CHAPTER-10

The Arrogant Tribe Pagañ-Pali Tribe

Told by: Hage Apa,HGB

Compiled by: Gyati Rana.

Long ago, the various clans of Apatani embarked on migration in different groups and routes to Sülo-Supuñ in the Ziro Valley from Müdo Supuñ. The villagers of Hari traversed the Kuru River and ventured through Pyuchi-Pyutü, Pyuda Sügya, Mipu Kormañ, and Talya Gyaso, eventually entering the valley from the western foothill. From there they moved towards the eastern hill via Tari Lembo and crossed paths with the Hüchi people who entered through Siya Gorge, the northeast side of the valley at present Hari Rantü.

The Hüchi clans, including Bamin, Michi, Mudang Tage, Hüja, and Duta, followed the Chillañ migration route from the east side of the Valley. They entered Ziro through Siya Gorge at the northeast of present Hari. They bypassed the colossal Shu Taru and unimpeachable Pigge Poro. They migrated further via Pyuli and Tadu Dobi and settled in the western foothills where Dübo Villages now stand.

Meanwhile, the courageous people of Hari, known for their diligence, cut down the colossal Shu Taru, the giant creeper spreading from Rantii at the North of Hari Village to

Pengu, the eastern entrance of Tadu and Dutta village and cleared the once untameable Pigge Poro and constructed the Dokañ La'pañ, their community platform.

As all Apatani clans united in the valley, they aimed to settle together at Bürü for safety; however, internal moral and ethical issues led to their dispersal to their earlier original occupied lands.

Indigenous Apatani culture spontaneously evolved in the early epoch of Üpyo. It reached its zenith in the epoch of Müdo. Throughout their migrations, the Apatanis preserved their culture and traditions holding the Myokó Festival, Muruñ ceremony and other rituals. They pull (Babo) Big Trees and La'pang, big platen logs from the deep jungle, erect that big tree as Baboo, an epitome of the Myokó festival and construct Lapañ with platen logs as a public platform in the middle of the Village. Therein, they perform Myokó Festival, Subu and Muruñ ceremonies to ensure the healthy progression and advancement of humanity, in particular, the community.

Many tribes and other clans desired to settle in the beautiful and prosperous Ziro Valley. Before the war with the Pagan-Lalyang and Pali-Lango tribe, a huge clan from the neighbouring Nyishi Tribe attempted to drive away the Apatani from the Ziro Valley. They came through a path called Püya Lembo at Tapañ Gambü, the northeastern ridge of the Valley.

Early in the morning, they reached Dusu-Katu, a viewpoint at the top of a hill from where one can have a bird's view of Ziro Valley. Normally, in the early morning, the Ziro Valley is covered by dense fog making it look like a huge lake.

The troop reached Dusu Katu early in the morning and they saw that dense fog below and misunderstood the morning fog as a huge body of water. They presumed that

Apatani and its Valley had been submerged in water and the valley had been turned into a lake. They told themselves that the people of Apatani were drawn underwater and the Valley had been turned into a huge Lake. There is no reason to attack them as they could not settle under the lake. So, they left without waging a war for their place.

It is said that they came and returned dragging their spears. Their number was so huge that many big roots of old wild Trees on their marching paths were cut into two due to the friction caused by the dragging of their spears.

Later, Pagañ-Lalyañ (one thousand population of strong clan, Pagan) and Pali-Lango (five hundred population of strong clan, Pali) also migrated through eastern Tapañ Ridge. They settled at two hillocks called Pagañ Putu and Pali Putu on the east side of the Hari village. Initially, the people of Hari village and these two clans had cordial relations like good neighbours. They used to visit the Hari village during the Myokó festival and Muruñ ceremonies. Hari people welcomed them to enjoy the delicacies of the festivals and sent them back with festival gifts.

As told earlier, the population of Hari village at that time was small compared to both, the Pagañ and Pali tribes. It had only around a hundred-plus households. Yet they had occupied and cultivated upon the huge fertile plain called Pigge Poro. They were self-sufficient in food grains. Every villager had two grain-filled granaries called Suchi and Suro. In those days, the granaries were constructed from Bamboo with grass roofs, one can easily open the roof and see the grains of the granaries. The people from Pagan and Pali saw the abundance of food grain and the fertile land of Pigge Poro, seeing these their greed and jealousy conquered their sense of friendship.

When the people of Hari had harvested their paddy and stocked them in their granaries, at pagan polyañ, the top of Pagan Hillock, the people of Pagañ and Pali set a Mell and decided to drive away the people of Hari Village and occupy their fertile land of Pigge Poro for themselves. Proud of their population, they were boasting that the countable people of Hari would stand nowhere in a war between them. They are nothing against the thousand-strong Pagan and five-hundred-strong Pali. The meagre Hari people were like feathers to them and could be easily blown away by a puff.

Accordingly, one fine day early in the morning, their leader, Pyagañ Tatañ came to Hari village with a group of people from Pagan and Pali. They gathered at Dokañ La'pañ, a public platform in the middle of the Village. He summoned the people of Hari and declared-

"Listen, you people of Hari, we the people of Pagan and Pali planned to settle here in your village and own your fertile Pigge Poro. For that, we are ready to wage war with you. You, the people of Hari, cannot stand against one thousand strong Pagans and Five hundred strong Pali. Therefore, we have come here to suggest you leave your village at your earliest or otherwise, we, the people of Pagan and Pali will drive you away like this feather." Saying this he took out a small feather and blew it away.

They were so overconfident that they earmarked the granaries and other properties they would take over after driving away the people of Hari. Their arrogance led them to even claim to snatch the wives of the Hari people.

The people of Hari in those days were war-hardened with hostile clans and tribes in their migration routes. Courageous and experienced in hunting, ambushing techniques and other war strategies. They may be small in population yet they decided not to run away but to fight back.

It is said that Müdo Kaga had a well-built body and strength of around five men. He had earned warring and fighting experience from his previous combat wars. He initiated and led the movements against Pagañ and Pali and called a meeting of warriors and strategists of Hari village like Hadañ Gyalañ, Pura Ro'po, Lyagi Melyang, Siigan Ro'po and Dinkhu Papu. Müdo Kago said in the Meeting, "This fertile land was infested by Colossal wild rope, Shu Taru and impeccable bushes at the swampy plain, Pigge Poro was occupied by our forefathers. No one but our forefathers dared to cut down those colossal wild ropes, clear the impeccable wild grass and hunt down the ferocious wild boar, Pige Siire, and occupy it. Pagañ Lalyañ and Pali Lango wish to settle here by driving us away. I do not wish to leave this place and run away. What do you suggest friends?"

Miido Kago continued, "The situation is serious, they even have earmarked our properties and assets like granaries for themselves. Due to our lesser numbers, it is obvious that we cannot defeat them in the war field. We need to work out some other tricks. Why not ambush them by preparing rice beers and inviting them to drink and later when they leave the village drunk and intoxicated, we can kill them" Kago Asked.

"Where and how will we ambush and kill them?" Hadañ Gyalañ Asked. "There is only one path to enter and exit our village. It is from Pato-chatu on the northeastern side the path is long and narrowest at Tar Lantiñ. Let us ambush them there and kill one by one who returned drunk." Sügan Ro'po suggested. All agreed on the proposal by Müdo Kago and Sügang Ro'po. Accordingly, they resolved to invite them to feed them and when they returned drunken, only to ambush them at Tar-Lanting.

In those days, the present Lüga and Gübü footpath was not yet open, and it was infested with impeccable bushes that even small animals could not go through. The present Pige-Lembo was non-existent. The only path used was from Pato-Chatu, which was too narrow at a point called Tar Lantiñ. Only a person could cross either by coming or going.

The people of Hari village sent a message to Pagan-Pali that they didn't want war with them. So, they will vacate their settlement for them. But before that, they wish to organize a Myokó-like Festival so that the people of Hari and Pagan-Pali could enjoy beers and delicacies as a farewell feast. Pagan-Pali happily accepted this proposal and agreed to participate in the farewell feast. The people of Hari enacted a special Myoko festival for Pagan and Pali and prepared rice beer from the available stock of their rice grains. Every household prepared rice beer, slaughtered animals for meat etc. When their setup to ambush was ready, they intimated and invited the Pagan and Pali people for a farewell feast.

On D-day, every person of Pangañ and Pali including children and women carrying their babies came to Hari via Paato Chato through narrow passage Tar Lanting. Delicious Beers and meats were prepared abundantly. All the guests were accommodated in various houses around the village and provided beer and meats to eat. While serving them they told them to eat and drink to the content of their hearts and minds and enjoy freely as villagers will vacate the village tomorrow for them.

Listening to such words while drinking sweet beer, the imagination to settle in Hari village increased their excitement. Out of enthusiasm, every one of them got drunk. Though they came in groups, when intoxicated with the rice beer they started leaving the village one by one without caring for each other through Tar Lantiñ, the only narrow path. As planned, they were ambushed and killed one by one at Tar Lantiñ, the narrowest portion of the path and their bodies were stacked and hidden in the designated place. The whole Pagan and Pali people were slaughtered except their leader who did not return.

When intoxicated with the rice beer they started leaving the village one by one without caring for each other through Tar Lantin, the only narrow path. As planned, they were ambushed and killed one by one at Tar Lantin, the narrowest portion of the path.

Pyagañ Tatañ, the Leader of Pyagan-Pali was hosted by Müdo Kago. He was enjoying the feast like a foodie. When Müdo Kago found that Pyagañ Tatañ was the only guest left in the village still feasting in his house, he started a quarrel with Pyagañ Tatan to kill him at his home. Both were physically well-built and veteran warriors; both tossed each other and even broke the floor in many places. Even after a long duel, Miido Kago could not kill him.

Every Apatani woman in those days was an expert weaver. In those days many solid pieces of wood called Dutiñ were available in every house. It was used multipurpose as a cotton ginning tool to separate the cotton seeds or as a sitting tool or pillow.

While both Pyagañ Tatañ and Müdo Kago were wrestling with each other, Kago's wife took Dutiñs and crashed the scrotums of Pyagañ Tatañ killing him instantly and ending their duel.

Later the bodies of Pagañ and Pali killed in the ambush were disposed of at different locations in Hari Village. There is a place northwest of Hari Village called Diñkhu, which means Skull. It is believed that all the heads of killed Pagañ and Pali were buried there. Another swampy place in the southwest of the village called Hapu, which means Hearth where all the Hearts of killed Pagan-Pali were buried, and all their hands and legs were thrown and buried at a place called Lüga, which means limbs. Still, these places in Hari village are known by these names.

Even after the victory a few decades back, the vengeful spirits of Pagañ-Pali used to hunt the village and cause stomachaches to the residents whose spirits are law. Nyibus, the Shaman had to perform the Gyalañ ritual to subdue those vengeful spirits alike with the "Ro'pi", a ritual of subduing the vengeful spirit of clawed and toothed animals killed in hunting.

They chant a hymn with a rhythm like, "Chuku da Tayu, Chubi da Tayu" while blowing horns weaving their swords and going up to the gyalañ-polyañ, the place where the Gyalañ altar is situated. And subdue the vengeful spirit of Pagañ-Pali who harms the residents.

To this day, the people of Hari village proudly recount the tale of their triumph over the mighty Pagañ-Lalyañ and Pali-Lango clans, solidifying their place as the victors in securing the Ziro Valley.

CHAPTER-11

Notorious Ziro People

Narrated by: Hage Apa

Compiled by: Gyati rana

The Apatani people migrated from Müdo Supuñ to their present location via various migration routes and settled in the foothills of the Ziro Valley. Upon reaching the valley, they encountered a group of people living on a hillock called Ziro Putu, on the northwest side of the current advanced airfield. These people, known as Ziro Miyu, were tattooed like the Apatani but wore different attire called "Hu'rriñ" and "Sabbe" similar to the Nyishi tribe

Since ancient times, the Apatanis have diligently preserved their unique culture and traditions, including festivals like Myokó and Muruñ, and marriage ceremonies like Mida and Eli. In the past, the Mida (marriage ceremony) was a grand affair known as "Dalo Mida, Salo Assa," where brides were selected from distant villages to showcase the ceremony far and wide. However, nowadays, this practice is fading away. Now, people started to choose their brides from within the village clans and sometimes from close clans.

The people of Ziro, with their larger population, began to harass the Apatanis by kidnapping their young women and committing heinous acts. They even disrupted the Mida ceremony by snatching away the brides. The Apatanis, intimidated by the sheer numbers of the Ziro people, felt powerless to stop these atrocities, which only encouraged the aggressors further. During the Penü procession of the Muruñ festival, unmarried Ziro women forcefully took Apatani men as their husbands.

The people of Ziro, with their larger population, began to harass the Apatanis by kidnapping their young women and committing heinous acts.

One tragic incident involved Dusu Suka Papu, a newly married woman, who was forcefully taken by an elder among Ziro people called Ziro Murchi during her journey back from the marriage ceremony. Similarly, Tanyang Sala Mado was also abducted by Ziro Murte during another Mida (marriage ceremony). The helpless Apatani men and Mida teams were unable to protect their wives or brides due to the overwhelming numbers of the Ziro people.

Feeling helpless and distraught, Dusu Suka Papu and Tanyang Sala Mado sought solace in the Kiilye River, where they played the Mipu Elu, a flute made from straw and expressed their sorrow through Büsi (folk Song) in forlorn tunes. Their song reached Cha-Doha, Küdi-Yapuñ and Doji-lyapuñ the spirits of the Earth, Sky, and terrestrial and jungle gods, who shed tears out of compassion that turned into a devastating rainstorm, ruining the paddy fields in the valley. Whole ripened grains were washed away.

The continuous harassment from the Ziro people pushed the Apatani to their limit, as their livestock and domestic animals like cows, Mithun, dogs, pigs, chickens etc. were not safe, and movement between villages was fraught with danger.

In a village meeting, the Apatani communities decided to unite and drive the Ziro people away for the safety of their people. They planned a coordinated attack, laying traps with poisonous bamboo spikes in trenches surrounding their villages. Ziro People proud of their numbers were confident that Apatani would not dare to attack them. However, they made bounds and spread thorny chestnut cover all over the entrance point of their village.

The Apatanis were a bit cleverer, they knew that it was dangerous to attack and fight them in their village. They dug numerous trenches around their villages planted sharp bamboo spikes with poison on them and concealed them with hays and leaves. When the day arrived, the Apatanis launched a successful assault on the periphery of the Ziro village and ran back to their respective villages. This assault enticed them to chase after them. The clever Apatani led the unaware Ziro people to their traps. All of the chasing Ziro people fell into the trenches and met their demise through the poisonous spikes. Those who did not participate in the war and survived also ran away.

Thus, the united efforts of the Apatani villagers resulted in the expulsion of the troublesome Ziro people from their land.

CHAPTER-12

Evolution of Ovomancy and Haruspicy in Apatani Society.

Do you know how the custom of ovomancy (reading signs through eggs) and haruspicy (reading signs through livers) evolved in the Apatani Society? Why such foreseeing was needed?

The evolution and practice of ovomancy and haruspicy in Apatani society have a fascinating story that sheds light on why foreseeing the future was considered crucial in their life.

As per Miji-Miguñ, the oral tradition of the Apatani people, the practices of ovomancy and haruspicy were not mere superstitions but ancient traditions of great significance. The genesis of these practices can be traced back to the legendary figure Abotani, the first human.

It begins from the day Abotani was born through "Chama Lyego" and "Doma Lyego", the door of Earth and the Sky respectively. The spirits, elements and animals were his elders as they were born earlier. He found himself in a challenging world filled with elements, spirits such as Akum-Pemo and Ayo-Khabo, and wild animals like Tage-Turo and Rama-Hirung, the wild boars. The constant threats of birds like Dodiñ-Müchi and Doko-Mülo, the Hawks and Eagles made his survival difficult.

He had no sharp Teeth like wild boars; Rama-Hiruñ and Tage-Turo or claws and beaks like hawks and eagles; Khonkhuñ-Dübo and Pyaro-Müche. He was so vulnerable, that even the spiky material around him easily pierced him. Lacking guidance and physical protection, Abotani realised the importance of understanding the intentions of others to make wise and informed decisions.

Amidst this backdrop of peril and uncertainty, his sister, Dolyañ Chanjañ, turned to the Eternal Guide Müdo Popi for help. Müdo Popi told her that Goddess Murtu and Hintü had the sacred eggs (Ra) and chickens (Yalyañ) that held mystical powers; Charé-Doré and Tapyu-Tabyo bestowed by the divine Gods Donyi and Shü. He suggested seeking Goddess Murtu and Hintü to bless them with those chickens and eggs and taught her the hymns of foreseeing. Accordingly, she told her brother Abotani about the sacred chickens and eggs and taught the foreseeing hymns she learned from eternal guide, Müdo Popi.

Abotani sought these eggs and chickens, imbued with sacred energies from the sun and the terrestrial gods, Goddess Murtu-Hintü. It became an instrument of insight and divination for Abotani. After chanting the appropriate hymns upon the chickens and studying the intricate patterns and designs in the egg yolks and livers, Tani could peer into the intentions of the spirits, elements, and creatures that roamed the land.

As Abotani delved deeper into the mysteries of ovomancy and haruspicy, he unearthed hidden truths and profound revelations that guided his every step and decision. The ancient practices became a beacon of wisdom in the darkness, offering him clarity in times of confusion and protection in moments of peril and suffering.

Since then, the Apatani people embraced ovomancy and haruspicy as sacred traditions passed down through generations. The rituals became a bridge between the mortal realm and the supernatural, providing a channel for communication with the unseen forces that shaped the world.

Since then, the Apatani people embraced ovomancy and haruspicy as sacred traditional passed down through generations. The rituals became a bridge between the mortal realm and the supernatural, providing a channel for communication with the unseen forces that shaped the world.

To this day, the echoes of Abotani's journey resonate in the hearts of the Apatani people, reminding them of the enduring legacy of ovomancy and haruspicy as pillars of wisdom and enlightenment in a world shrouded in supernatural mystery.